KĀLĪ

The Invocative Poems
of Ramprasad Sen

Newly translated into
modern street English

by
Moulee de Salm-Salm
&
Caiyros Arlen Strang

AmunCiné
Wells - Pierce
Boston - Cambridge
2016

OM KRIM KALIKAYEI NAMAHA

Introduction

WHO WAS RAMPRASAD SEN?

Rāmprasād Sen (c. 1718 or ca. 1723 – c. 1775)
was a Shakta poet who lived in Bengal. His
many poems were simply known as Pamprasadi
and they are all poems either directly or
indirectly said and written or written down later
– to the Goddess Kali.
His life story is based upon legends and hearsay
remembrances of people who knew him and/or
were told about him. His poems have been
repeated and written down from many sources.
Ramprasad was born in the village of Halisahar,
on the banks of the Ganges, thirty-five miles
north of Kolkata, into a Tantric Vaidya-Brahmin
family. His father, Ramram Sen, was a Sanskrit
scholar and an Ayurvedic doctor. His mother,
Siddheswari was the second wife of His
father.Siddheswari was Ramram's second wife.
Young Ramprasad was educated at a Sanskrit
school, where he not only studied the classical
Sanskrit tol (school) where he learned Sanskrit
grammar, literature, and the Persian and Hindi
languages. He began writing poetry as a child,
and yong Ramprasad was also a disciple of the
Tantric scholar, Agamavisha. Later in life he
became the court poet for King Krishna Chandra
of Nadia. Ramprasad is believed to have
written: Vidyasundar; Kali-kirtana; and
Shaktigiti. Also, he created a new form of poet
song that is a combnination the Bengali folk
music of Baul with classical music and the
kirtan, and which became very popular.

Ramprasad married and later worked as an
accountant, but his devotion to Kali was such
that he even wrote hymns to Kali in the account
books. His boss finding this out, read the poems
and was so moved by them that he told
Ramprasad to go back to his village and to write

more of his devotional poetry to Kali, and that he would keep Ramprasad on salary for as long as he (the boss) lived.

Ramprasad returned to his village and regular practiced Sadhanan in a pnachavati – a grove of 5 trees – a banyan, a bael, an amakaki, and a peepu;. These groves are specifically used in certain tantric practices. Also he performed sadhanas while standing neck-deep in the Ganges water, all the time singing songs to the Goddess Kali.

It was village legend often appeared to Ramprasad Sen that Kali in her form of Adyasshakti Mahamaya, which is a combination of many different life and events of super-nature. These elements are: Adi Shakti, is the energy-power for the manifestation of the Cosmos as it first becomes Ardhanarishwara.who is the Hermaphrodite form of Prajapati as Shiva.

Adi shakti , then creates Yoga Maya, and this gives limitless forms (all with individual names) to the 3 distinct forms: Brahmaa, Vishnu and Mahesh, and have the complete knowledge of Yoga Maya as well as being able to embody it.a.

Yoga Maya creates a balance of Vishnu, the Preserver, with Shiva the Destroyer.

Then , there is an apparent reversal of power and energy, Vishnu the Preserver actually takes Yoga Maya to create Maha Maya.

Maha Maya creates the Devas , but does not revel to the Devis – their own True Self Nature – thus forcing them to think and act, in their own form, their own name, and the duties formed by such advanced karmic structures. Thus, Indra is forced to think that He, Indra IS Indra and be the duty of USE to take care of all natural elements such as, on Earth, rain, growing plants, and so on.

MahaMaya (Divine Illusion) then creates Maya, which makes the souls (egos) and envelop them into her bossom, and force them forget they are divine or they are Brahmm

Maya can be overcome by meditation and Mantra

MahaMaya can be overcome by hard penance / tapas and this penance can only be done by those who have already overcome Maya Yoga Maya is independent of all means of coercion, force of patterns, and thus entirely free, except for certain aspects of her own acts of desire that are entirely Herself, rather than a karma, an attitude, or a way of thinking, and Her own desire is to release Herself from Herself while still maintaining Herself as Herself.

Ramakrishna Paramahamsa (February 18, 2836 – August 16, 1886) guru to Swami Vivekananda (January 12, 1863 – July 4,m 1902) guru to Dhyanyogi Mahasudundas Ji (1878 – August 29, 1994) guru to Asha Macreated a chain of people who saw and see Ramprasad Sen's poetry as holy words.

Sister Nivedita (1867-1911): Student of Swami Vivekananda has compared Ramprasad's street slang conversational holy poems to the poetic illuminations of the English poet William Blake.

Moulee de Salm-Salm
Caiyros Arlen Strang
March 30, 2016

Mother
I live in the slum-hut I built from my own fear.

Winds from the sky shake it.
Winds from my own mind
shake it

But I say Your Name and You Preserve that part
of my dwelling that preserves me.

Holy Mother,
Each and every night
Six Thieves
Made of
lust, anger, greed, pride, envy, and sloth

climb my battered crumbling walls to sneak into
me.

I cannot fight these thieves alone, Holy Mother,
so I run while I stay
And stay while I run

As Ramaprasad,
I pray:
Let me not
be a prisoner
within limitations
found to be
the exterior of
My own dwelling.

Oh My Mind,
let you be,
to stay stable,
And aware,
singing softly, "Kali-ma, Kali-ma".

Fool! While Awake,
do not sleep
The fortunes
You do have now.

And when you
lay your gentle,
breathing body,
Down,

Guard the nine openings
Of your own "You"

From those unpleasant forces who can enter
All the lives you live,
And steal, anything, everything,
Whatever!
your nine real openings
from body to soul
to steal whatever is left to take!

3

You are
sleeping that sleep
of desire
in the final bed of Time,
holding itself in this world.

You are
thinking no dawn can come
to cancel pleasure;
In the ending night,
your familiar mistress
lies by you.

But You
Have become
worn out
By many stupid actions.
You cannot turn to see Her.
You cannot bathe in Her
You hide your face
under the sheets
of random hopes
And the desire to act as stupidly
As others,
Who do not even like you.

Winters go
Summers come
Summers go
And winters come again.

Come again.
Go again.
Come again.
Go again.

The bed sheet remains unwashed.

You only drink the wine,
Of your one world,

And you cannot stop.

Night, dawn, day, and dusk
You're drunk within
A very small world inside of worlds.
End this narrowness!

Call Kali's Name.

4

What a fool you are, Ramaprasad.

Hope is not the food for sleep.
And sleep is not the food for hope,

Do not wait for or praise deeper sleep to come
to you

when you are called
and called again,
nevermore to wake
or answer,

and yet you live still.

5

Ramaprasad says:
Oh mind of mine
Please do not sleep!

Let time not break into me
And steal from me,
And all that is me within.

You let me touch and hold,
Your Holy Sword,
Mad from the Holy Lingham which You,
Yourself
Made hard.

Mother Kali!
I build out from Your Name.

I hold daughter Tara's name as I would hold
Your Shield.

Can you be overcome by Death Itself?

It has been written so,
This writing is a horn
That sounds Kali's name.

And Kali's Mother?

Chant Durga! Durga! Durga!
Chant! Chant! Chant, until Dawn reaches you.

Will She save me,
In this Great Dark Age,
Almost, but not yet over?

7

Aha, but so many weaknesses
continue in safety!

Am I safe?

Mother! Mother!
Mother! Mother!

Does suffering
actually
bring me
into fear?

I do suffer!
I do require more?
I do carry
suffering upon my head.
I do try
to sell it from my stall in this bazaar of living life
Of everyone and everywhere.

I do live
on poison internally carried.
All of it - wherever I go.

Ramaprasad says:
Mother! Mother!
 I need rest.

Amazing fools we are;
Some brag of happiness,
while I brag of suffering!

Why do we each do this?
Why? Mother! Why?

About illusion -
Well, there's a power and a goddess and a magic
lantern show -

Where we are as the strangest of the strange
within all -

Beings trapped within illusion
Who quickly move as infinite patterns
yet, not one pattern is truly seen as the next
pattern has already arrived.

Free beings
form themselves
from within contentment.

"I am this or that..."
"This or that is one part of me..."
Merely, these are the forms of stupid thinking!

O Mind, Yourself,
in the ceaseless, seizing, careless tangle
You place within the human heart,
You do believe that all is real!

"Who am I...?"
"What who is mine...?"
"Is any or all else real...?"

O Mind,
who is servant,
who is served?

My own gladness
and sadness
dissolve.

O Mind - why do you let yourself become
A light within a dark room -
made gone by what is in it!

Finally,
we grasp what we lose,
By not grasping it all,
But by being in the realm that holds it.

One must be careful in one's Wise-House!
Wise Guy!

Ramaprasad says:
Lift that mosquito net -
See the Self!
See it Now?

11

Go on!
You simple-minded death-lover
I am the son of Kali, my She's my Mom!

Ask your Lord:
Has he welcomed with kindness,
many like me?

With Kali's Light,
stable within my mind,
I can be the death of death,
And will be.

Ramaprasad says:
Servant, servant, listen!

Do not bad-mouth,
In silence or in yelling
out here!

If you are tied and bound
As flesh within
the net of Kali's Name,
and yet,
you are still defeated,
then who will save you
where and when?

O Death,
here I stand and
I've drawn a circle
round me and it was truly
made from Kali's Name.

That's all. Simple.
Easy to do.

When Shiva
plays The Great Death,
He has Kali stand
upon His sky-facing body.
Her feet stand on His heart
And then, sexually,
She mounts Him.

Remember!

Kali's feet
cancel all fear,

Who
now needs fear death ever!

I give my heart
to those feet,
The feet of
Terror's Destroyer.
Do I still fear Death?
Really?
Do I/
Really?

Kali's name
is the
wish-fulfilling tree
Growing at the center of all space.

Its live seeds
I carry within
my heart.

I've sold my bones
in markets,
in order to buy
Durga's Name.

I live in a house.
My self lives
in my flesh -
and elsewhere also!

When Death finally comes
to enter into my life,
I have decided to open my heart
and show Him all there is there!

Tara's Name
is the subtlest medicine.
Her name adorns all
my tied-up long hair.

Ramaprasad says:

Already I've begun my journey,
because I've called Durga's Name.

In this place,
what can I fear?

My body lies
within Tara's Body's Field
in which Holy Shiva
as God of Gods
becomes a Farmer
sowing His Seed
with the song mantra:
Om Namah Shivaya.

Faith is a fence
around His body.

Patience are the posts.

He drives Six Oxen,
Plowing into pleasure,

He cuts short
the blowing grass
with a Chopping Blade
When there is
Kali's Name.
Love is rain
Devotion, love
are night and day.

Ramaprasad he says:

On the tree of Kali
all you need and do
is pick for yourself.
Then all good
and pleasant things
become release,
Not prison.

Please tell me,
My brother -
what happens after death?

The whole world is asking about it!
And they argue about it, too !

They say:
In death we
become a ghost or spirit
or something
And then go to heaven!

They say you
can live closer
to Some God in some way.

And the Vedas tell us,
you are a reflection of the sky,
mirrored out from a clay unpainted water jar,
soon to shatter!

You see
sin and virtue
within nothing
and nothing is your reward.

Many elements interrelate
within our bodies.

At death,
these elements separate.

Ramaprasad says:
My brother,
you end where you begin;
merely, strongly
a reflection rising from water,
mixing with waters,
and at one with water.

And still alive.

Death do not touch me!
Now, I am without social status
because it is a day
of Mother Kali's kindness.

Death, listen!
To You I will tell the story.
My Beloved Dark Destroyer
made me turn from family life to begging.

My heart and voice
joined to sing
sweet Kali's Name.
And those Six Passions
of lust and anger,
greed and pride,
envy and sloth,
heard my song and slunk away.
I am here
and still hold the power of an outcast.

Ramaprasad says:
When the outcast dies,
Death will be far away.

Tender, pitying Mother,
do I ever truly, actually worship Thee
from the free will that is mine?

Would anyone worship You,
if you made Death's Terror void?

Mother,
where are You
whose strength is all;
the first original power?

Your name only - is freedom,
You - Goddess of Three Forms of Many Gazings
at Once!

Where did I go wrong?

You know each day seems harder.

I sit and cry in this kind of time.
I tell myself to leave this life.
I've had too much of all this.

As a good servant stays busy,
Shiva is the Lord of Death,
And came inside me,
and spun the wheel of Times and Actions.

So I say, I am getting out into life.
I abandon all but Kali's Name.
But You, personally addicted me,
You personally, made me make that love
That goes to all the great things of this –
Your Great World!

You know!
I can never let it go!

At the dust beneath Kali's feet,
Ramaprasad cries out:

Dark Goddess,
I am caught in a motion of shadows,
born of Your Dark World's Many Moods
In Your One Mood.

O Kali-ma,
what are the limits of Your capabilities?

Mad Girl, Mad Woman, Mad Old Lady - All!
You trick us to see the madness.

No one knows the Other,
in your built world inside Your created illusions
inside of Truth.

Kali's tricks
are skill beyond content.

And upon this skill,
we are invited to dance.

It is crazy suffering, Crazy Girl!
Who knows really Who or What She Is?

Ramaprasad says:
One kind decision from Her
makes her kindness
Make all miseries pass away, away, and away...

My mind dreams in image rhythms.
Are the nurturing breasts of Kali clay or image?
This type of mind labor wastes my strength.

Can clay or any image
cool a running, groaning, grunting mind?

So Her skin is either red or black.
She holds a sword
and wears a necklace made of dry skulls or fresh
heads.

Yet Her eyes are the Sun
and Her eyes - the hidden-fire Moon.

No one can create those eyes but Her.
Clearly Kali severs evil.
No stupid image does this!

She wipes clean my mind
to show Herself to me.

She plays inside my heart.

Whatever I think,
it is within her Name.

I close my eyes
and see her.

That human heads garland
frames Her breasts, belly, crotch, and knees.

Common sense?
long gone!

Some say I'm crazy.

Let them all
do this,
I don't care.

Crazy Kali,
stay by me.

Ramaprasad cries to you:
Kali-ma don't pass
from my lotus heart
you live within.

Don't dislike me
as I peek at your sexual nakedness
and look up
from the bottom
of Your feet.

O my mind!
Do you still fall in love
with your single, shifting fantasy?

Kali is there.
You stare and fail to see Her.
Our universe itself, is one image
within Our Kali's Mind.

You know it!
Why not believe it too?
And why do I look for Her
as an image of worship?
As, any inmage of worship?

24

My mind
was a gambler
who gambled
and lost.

All moves
of the mind
are a gamble.

Yet awake,
I continue
to move!

Mind,
who do you console
and what
do you
have?

Your body
is a
tube.
grinding
ocean
wet sand.

Move.
Lightly
as
a
wind
sail.

Kali
is
your
teacher.

Move
lightly.

Move
within
your own
passion
and
Your own darkness,
now.

What do you think I am?
A premature baby?

I will never give You up.
No matter what expression
You shall stare
into my eyes!

Why tease me and trick me
When I've given myself
to have you here.

Shiva's mantra:
"Om Namah shivaya"
is the promise of You
delivered and sealed within my heart.

Now Shiva's
absolute justice comes!
In the Court of Karma,
You shall see me
demanding You.

Shiva has
given me
the path
of future history
and its leading only
to You.

Ramaprasad says:
This legal contest
shall amaze all beings.
There is no settlement until
You hold me lovingly as You.

Hope lives
in hope -
a happening
again happening.

A bee blunders
into
the painted
lotus.

You give
me bitter leaves to bite

sworn sweet to
and my addict's love
of cold sugar.

It makes me drool
poison
which never kills.

Kali-ma
to this world
You lured me.

"Let's play",
You say.

But You left me
alone in a game,
not really begun.

Ramprasad knew this
in your presence.

Now take me
in your arms
And hold me
within Your home.

I wont call You anymore,
You Crazy Girl!

I won't call You,
Crazy Kali!

Who carries Her sharp sword into battle,

always naked from the flex of Your nipples
to Your holy feet.

You give something.
You take something.
And it is always soon!

Why do You spoil this half-wit boy,
Kali-Ma?

Ramaprasad says:

You've done it now!

Once I was an empty floating thing.
Now You've filled me with so much life,

I'm a full bucket,

sunk floating
below the water line.

One, Insane Woman!

Stop standing
on Shiva's groin.

He is not dead.
this eternal-wisdom force
is giving us meditation.

We pretend:

He is weak
from poison.

We pretend :

He cannot bear
the force of Kali's foot.

Get off of Him!
Before You break
His unbreakable ribs.

He drinks poison and lives.

Well?
Why should He die!

And now Ramaprasad says:

He plays with sleep
and death,
just to tease from You,
all and everything that
Your touching feet
Bring Him.

Dear One,

You!
Live naked without shame.

You !
Live as the naked Queen.

Kali-ma!
In great seriousness,
You stand on Shiva's chest.
All of You moves naked
in this burning grave of human bodies on fire.

O Kali-ma!

Wear Your female ornaments!

Wear Your gleaming necklace
of shining human heads!

Wear your illuminations
on ornaments of bones from dead bodies!

Ramaprasad says:

We all feel fear of You.
Your power as You,
Shiva fears as well,
in this, Your current mood,
where all structure
in the wrath of violence
is projected out, made manifest, and
simultaneously
self-swallowed by You
as unendurable
compassion
endured
forever.

Who else? Who else?
But You can do this?

Please Kali!
Continue Your deceptions.
I am undeceived,
at rest with Your feet
bringing calm to me
as that old trembling cringe
called fear leaves me.

I am light
grown from passions.

I no longer live
in my own poisoned well.

Pleasure and pain are the same;
all burned within my mind;
smothered out and gone.

No more drinking
of that certain wine which brings those
certain desires
which led us
into begging
door to door to door.

No more breathing
that certain wind of hope
which leads those inner methods
of my heart
into the streets
of numb, collapsing talk.

No more tangling in
the trick drizzle-dazzle
which hangs as
a senile demon on
the tree of love.

34

Ramaprasad says:

Can you add milk to milk
and make that simple taste,
Taste more pure?

Why look for a river
and a giver of eternal life?

I sing my Beloved's Name.

Why leave my home
when my home is my Beloved?

And I cease to be, anything but Her?

Ramaprasad says:

Who calls to You as lover
when the only caller
calls to You
as You?

Kali-ma!

You are more beautiful
than more of anything.

Your wilding hair blows
through the wilderness of wind.

Your Self-willed body is stripped
of socially built fears I call "Clothing of clothing".

Your earrings from children
are the crossroads of immortality,
Made of changing, and sound.

Your necklace of human heads
are really clustered lights
(You know this!)
of conscious worlds
bouncing against your sweating skin.

Your jigging breasts
are the waves of energy
breaking open the closed track of time which
fools believe to be time itself.

Your belt of severed hands
are the mind's genital powers
creating time through touching space.

Your thighs' heats
are the desire to live made necessary.

Your feet walk
on the very body of death
and show it to be the illusion of worry
within the changing patterns of desire
within the dance of all unbearable beauty.

Ramaprasad says:

Your lips are jasmine;
the pure and simple.

And Your face
has no description.

Each time You laugh,
a lotus blossoms
somewhere.

Your dark body
boils the very thickness
Of air
in the rain
from the rain
as dark rain falls
into night.

O my mind!
You bounce
in moods,
in love with Beauty;
Itself beyond
all further waking,
and beyond
all counted cost.

The fisherman
is casting his nets;
waiting and waiting.

Mother of Worlds:
In this world
ultimately, what will I be?

Fish swim free
in deep waters.

As a net
this world is cast
into ultimate space.

Mind itself -
do not accept
the question:
"What will you do?"

Kali-ma,
I know,
You can
manage this
problem.

Holy Devi Tara,
here is my story.

I live in a house of war
where five special senses play like children,
seeking the eternal pleasure
of full awareness.

I have lived
and I have been born
Into 8,000,000 forms of life,
and right now I am
a funny-looking man
carrying a partial gift.

Mother,
look at Ramaprasad.

He's a tenant
of a special house
whose ruler is made crazed
by babbling tenants
fighting each other
Among varied sexualities;
causing the five senses
to rage.

Holy Mother,
You are playing games again.
What do You take when You give?
What do You give when You take?

You make equal
all dusks and dawns.
You are a perfect freedom.
You cannot be stopped,
as "now" and "then", and "later",
are all the same to You.

Even Shiva
lying under You,
could forget
His own
present awareness
as His erect penis
grows into Your Time-Showering opening,
as
You show me
a stone floating on water
and i am
Your
son.

43

A cold stone
is not motherhood
and motherhood
is not
child's
play.

44

Today
always is passing.
So stories
live.

Woman of Stone,
glance back at me,
as I sing my songs of You,
In a realm of
Anyhow and anyway,
plunging into
the ocean of
this
world.

My Mother is found
in all and every house.

I stand and state this
in public places.

She is wrathful Bhairavi,
sexy, leg-entangled
with Shiva.

She is Durga
with her Shining Children.

She is sweet Sita
in the world of Vishnu.

My Holy Mother is
mother, daughter, sister, wife.

She is every woman.

Always is She close to you.

What more can Ramprasad say?
Work out your own personal details.
This are your hints for Today!

I've had my fun.

I used to make money making money.

Now I've stopped working daily jobs.

That time has passed.

My wife and children,
friends and brothers
would listen to me
when I spoke.

Now, they can't listen,
even when they try!

Poverty can equal death, you know.
Already, I see
my relations
stacking up the firewood
to burn the corpse
and do all their old, silly, boring rituals,

while they're even bored themselves.

Say "See ya around!"
to this old boy
in his fake holy costume.

And say: "Hari, Hara" too!
Then throw me to the flames
and walk off!

That's all for Ramaprasad
(So they say!)
Their tears magically dry
as they begin to eat their supper
(So I say!) OK!

Sing Her name,
sing Kali!

If someone whispers:
"He's another madman!"
Let 'em!

If someone attaches
harsh and ugly thoughts
to Your Name,
does it really matter?
Let 'em!

Good is not bad,
nor can it ever be!
Let 'em figure that one out!

With Kali's Name
hack and slash
these trash mountains
to an even flatness
within my life's geography.

In the good,
we live as good.

But Ramaprasad admit,
Your heart is full enough
To still voluteer to walk
the streets of this world.
heartsick,
cold,
and
alone.

Mountain Father Giri!

I can no longer bring comfort
to Your goddess-daughter Uma.

Crying
and making sad faces,
She won't suck a breast
or drink warm milk pudding.

The moon
speeds into the central night while
Uma begs
to hold the moon.

No mother calmly, can
see those wet eyes
and pale face.

She cries to me:
"Come, come, please, Mother."
She clutches
my smallest finger.
Where does She want to go?

"Is there a way
to capture the moon?"
I ask.

She throws
jewelry at me.

Mountain Father Giri
conforts goddess Gauri
Who sits upon His lap.

"Little Mother!" I say,
"Here! Have the moon!',
I hand her her mirror.

She sees her face
framed with glowing
in the silver backed glass.

Now happy.
Radiant and beyond
those energies of a million counted nights
of full
and
crescent
moons.

Shri Ramaprasad says:

A rich, man
in whose house, the Mother lives.
Can say
Only what I've now just said,
Watching as the Monn-watcher Lays
so gently
so very, very gently
asleep
in Her small firm
Bed.

Uma is
a most precious girl.
She is more than just daughter
to a Lord Mountain Father.

I fear my own knowledge,
but I'll tell it to you now.

Beneath our opaque surface of dreams

Uma becomes God with Four Faces

(and the Brahma Force of All hears this!)

From our awareness greater than
simply being awake,

Uma can become
The Great God with Five Faces
(Shiva sees!)
She is the Great Feminine Power
who attracts the God of Continuing
(Vishnu is here!)

Ramaprasad says:

Eternal Fortunate Mountain,
how did you acquire a daughter so fair.

To and from,
in either direction and both
She limits without even trying,
when the Holy Ones approach.

My daughter
cannot be
property of
another.

My heart
knows this.

Yet,
really,
I do not.

Sometimes,
I cannot stand
the bitter play
of uneven,
woven,
karmas.

Ramaprasad says:

Masculine Mountain
is alive through Feminine Fire.
Before they turn to One.

This is the pattern
for two birds
at dawn
in hunger
for their
moonlight.

Why should I travel
to a holy city
or seek to see
the holiest river?

Already,
I am
at the holy feet of Kali.

I meditate this,
with a rainbow lotus flower
at the center of my heart.

I walk the surface
of all water's bliss.

Her feet are the red lotus flowers.

Her feet are holy temples of enlightenment.

Her name, Kali, when spoken aloud,

Itself, burns evil into nothing,
within a safe, enduring fire.
And with Her
living in your mind,
there is no need to worry.

When I listen
to tales of sacred journeys,
those with genuine offerings,
hardships, and good deeds,
I laugh at your childish minds.

What good is a salvation
which saves one,
if it swallows you,
like water going into water?

Ramaprasad is amazed

and says:

Hold all grace and mercy coming
from Her own wilding hair.

Hey! Think about it!

And all the forms
Of "Good" & "True"
Bring themselves on!

Is it over, Mother?
Is all done?

As dust plays
in dust,

playing as a boy,
plays with a daughter
of Supreme Mountains,
is it?

Sometimes,
I get scared.

I see the games
to be more serious than I had thought,
(or, perhaps, could ever think).

Did I waste my pleasure
in my breath?

Could I have sung
better?

Where should my energy have gone,
going through this world?

Ramaprasad humbly asks:

My Mother!
Reach within and pull
my old age out
from that dusty, dirty dance of death!

Teach this lover love!

Now wash me in cleanest water
that only You know
is You

KALI:
EARLIEST KNOWN MENTIONS OF HER:

The word Kālī appears as early as the Atharv
Veda the first use of it as a proper name is in the
Kathaka Grhya Sutra (19.7)

Kali is the name of one of the seven tongues of
Agni, the [Rigvedic] God of Fire, in the Mundaka
Upanishad (2:4)

First appearance of Kālī in her present form is in
the Sauptika Parvan of the Mahabharata
(10.8.64). She is called Kālarātri (literally,
"black night") and appears to the Pandava
soldiers in dreams, until finally she appears
amidst the fighting during an attack by Drona's
son Ashwatthama She most famously appears in
the sixth century Devi Mahatmyam as one of the
shaktis of Mahadevi, and defeats the demon
Raktabija ("Bloodseed").

The Kalika Purana (!)th c.) worships Kālī as the
ultimate reality or Brahman.

Kālī is probably first mentioned in Hinduism as
a distinct goddess around 600 CE, and these
texts almost always place Her on the edges of
society rather than in the middle of society. Also
Kali is seen as a Warrior Goddess.

Within her many existences, Kali is often known
as the Shakt of the God Shiva and is closely
associated with him in some of the Puranass. In
the Kalika Purana she shows Herself as Adi
Shakti that is both primordial and also beyond
all nature (Para Prakriti).

Fin.

Made in the USA
Coppell, TX
28 June 2020

29480262R00039